Marcel Dassault
Mirage III

Pere Redón

Printed in The United States of America.
ISBN: 978-0-7643-4370-4

This book was originally published in Spanish under the title *Marcel Dassault Mirage III* by Reserva Anticipada Ediciones, Barcelona. ISBN: 84-95493-13-6

We are interested in hearing from authors with book ideas on related topics.

Published by Schiffer Publishing Ltd.
4880 Lower Valley Road
Atglen, PA 19310
Phone: (610) 593-1777
FAX: (610) 593-2002
E-mail: Info@schifferbooks.com.

Visit our web site at:
www.schifferbooks.com
Please write for a free catalog.
This book may be purchased from the publisher.
Try your bookstore first.

Marcel Dassault
Mirage III

Pere Redón

4880 Lower Valley Road   Atglen, Pennsylvania 19310

Acknowledgments

The author wishes to give thanks for the help received from the Public Relations Office of the Air Force Headquarters. Thanks also to the *Revista de Aeronáutica y Astronáutica*, and to General J. Vasco. A special mention to his friends José Nebreda, Gonzalo Ávila, and Roberto Yáñez, without whom this monograph would not have been possible.

Introduction

The aircraft which has had a starring role in the history of French aeronautical industry has undoubtedly been the Mirage III of Avions Marcel Dassault-Breguet Aviation, known today as Dassault Aviation. For a time, this aircraft dominated the world aeronautical market in the area of fighter aircraft, and it is still the European fighter plane which has been manufactured in the highest numbers.

The story of the Mirage came about as a consequence of the lessons learned during the Korean aerial war. When this ended, in 1953, the *Armée de l'Air* issued a document which contained the specifications for the design of a small, light aircraft capable of an ascent, when completely armed, to a height of 60,040 feet (18,300 meters) in less than six minutes. All the French aeronautical firms of this period responded to the call, with Dassault being the only one to put forward a project which offered a combined thrust. The engine had to have a conventional turbojet and a liquid propellant rocket, whose combination would allow for the climb requirements to be possible. This was how the MD 550 Mirage I came about, with its delta wing and propelled by two Armstrong Siddeley Viper turbojets (1,643 pounds/745 kilos each), built under license by Dassault, complemented by a ventral module —

El MD550-01, known as the Mystère. This was the first aircraft with a delta-wing by the French company Marcel Dassault. Note the large size of the rudder, which would later be altered. *(Dassault Aviation)*

The MD550-01 prototype, with the alteration of the rudder to a swept-back shape, the smaller French flag, and the word Mirage at the front. *(Dassault Aviation)*

disposable when finished — containing a 3,307-pound (1,500-kilo) thrust SEPR 66 rocket motor. This aircraft flew for the first time June 25 1955, whilst the aircraft with the jet flew in December 1956, attaining Mach 1.5 in level flight.

This aircraft, whose production did not go further than the prototypes, was a way of proving the validity of the delta design. These tests paved the way for the concept of a somewhat larger aircraft, a variation named the Mirage II, which had a propulsion engine formed of two Turbomeca Gabizo turbojets, each with 2,043-pound (1.090-kilo) thrust and 1,654-pound (750-kilo) rockets. Even with all the planned maximum velocity, it was only Mach 1.55, which was still less than the requirements, meaning that this aircraft did not progress past the planning stage. Nevertheless, the experience and the technology accumulated by the manufacturer meant that in a record time of nine months, the delta-wing developed was joined to a new fuselage design that was built around the most powerful engine available at that time, the SNECMA ATAR 101 G 1, with 9,921-pound (4,500-kilo) thrust, with afterburners and supported by a SEPR 66 rocket.

A Mirage IIIEZ on its way to South Africa in front of the production plant. The retouching of the photograph for publicity purposes with the roundel of Spain and the St Andrew's Cross indicates that it was taken in 1969, when contact was first made between the Air Force and Avions Marcel Dassault.
(*Revista de Aeronaútica y de Astronaútica*)

This was how the Mirage III came about, whose prototype (001) flew November 18, 1956. The mechanics baptized the aircraft with the telephone number Balzac 0001, which belonged to a famous French public relations agency at the time.

On January 20, 1957, Mach 1.5 reached an altitude of 36,089 feet (11,000 meters), and after a modification of the air intakes it managed to fly close to the official requirement at Mach 1.8.

At that time, the French manufacturers who were engaged in achieving the model required by the *Armée de l'Air* already had a number of interceptor aircraft in flight that used different combinations of propellants with various degrees of success, especially rockets with jets and ramjet with jets. The combination adopted for the Mirage III showed itself to be the most successful, and the one which allowed for an efficient interceptor capable of multiple roles that could not be achieved by other combinations.

Ten preproduction Mirage IIIA were ordered, the first of which took off May 12, 1958, reaching Mach 2.2 during this flight. All these aircraft were used in a great number of tests with the help of those that foreshadowed and

In the foreground, the first ten Air Force Mirage III at Dijon-Longvic base in April 1970. *(Revista de Aeronaútica y de Astronaútica)*

shaped the series version Mirage IIIC, with a SEPR 841 support rocket, Cyrano radar, drogue parachute, and missile-based armament.

Designed at the same time as this, there was the two-seater version called the Mirage IIIB, which was used for training. This model, with simplified equipment, was larger, in order to allow for a second seat to be fitted; this meant that part of the electronic equipment had to be reinstalled in the nose, which, in this version, meant it did not have radar. Its overall capacity was greatly reduced, even if it still maintained

suitability for combat, thanks to its internal armament of two cannons being retained.

The first one-hundred aircraft of the series began to be delivered to the *Armée de l'Air* October 9, 1960. The engine was the ATAR 9 B 3, with 9,370 pounds (4,250 kg) dry thrust and 13,228 pounds (6,000 kg) with afterburner. This model opened up the foreign market, as South Africa ordered the CZ version and Israel ordered the CJ version. The latter, adapted to local requirements, was built under license in that country by Israel Aircraft Industries (IAI).

Over the years, and with the accumulation of flight hours around the world, the Mirage III was modified, adapting it to the requirements of each particular time and situation, making it a very versatile and extremely multi-faceted model. Of all these, even though it did not reach the production stage, one version stands out for curiosity sake: the IIIV version, which was used in 1966 as a test bed for an aircraft with vertical landing and take off.

The Mirage III was made famous by its valiant contribution to the Six Days war in

1967, once again faced by Israel and the neighboring Arab countries. It also successfully participated in other conflicts, such as the 1971 Pakistan-India war. More recently, it was seen in action during the Falklands war in 1982. Updated according to requirements, it is still active in various air forces, mainly in South America.

The two supply sources

At the end of the 1970s, the aerial defense of Spain still fell to the antiquated North American F-86F Sabre and a reduced number of Lockheed F-104G Starfighters. It had been evident for a number of years that new aircraft needed to be incorporated to replace the old Sabre and finish the actions of the Starfighter, an aircraft which was very complicated to handle and difficult to maintain due to a widespread shortage of spare parts.

The Air Force, at that time under the command of Lieutenant General Julio Salvador Díaz Benjumea, was planning the diversification of its supply sources for aerial materiel, and also to stop its exclusive dependence on the

This Mirage IIIEE shares the runway at Manises with a number of T-33 aircraft and two AISA I-15, all in training. This indicates that the image was taken in the first few weeks after its arrival. *(Revista de Aeronaútica y de Astronaútica)*

C.11-1 flies over the port of Valencia on its return from a bombing training mission. It can be seen that the flap of the auxiliary air inlet behind the insignia of Ala 11 is open. *(Revista de Aeronaútica y de Astronaútica)*

United States. Since the signing of the U.S.-Spanish agreement of 1953, the U.S. had shown itself to be generous in the supply of leftover material, though it was not quite so generous when it came to its use, as shown in 1957 during the Ifni crisis. It was clear that the acquisitions policy needed changing and diversifying, with the best chance for this being that which was already planned, the replacement of the old flight material.

With a view to Spanish requirements, the experts from the Spanish Air Force planned the purchase of a number of Mirage III aircraft; Jaguar, the Franco-British fighter plane; the Swedish Draken; and the F-4 Phantom II. The first to be rejected were the Jaguar and the Draken, as they did not meet all the necessary requirements, leaving the Phantom on the back burner for another occasion a few months later. Interest centered on the French aircraft, which

were able to be quickly incorporated and could even be manufactured in Spain.

The first official contacts between the Air Force and the French manufacturer began in September 1969, when a committee of experts visited the Dassault factory, during which time the foundations for a possible acquisition agreement were laid down.

At the beginning of the 1970s, it became evident that the Spanish proposal included the

The two lower air brake flaps can be seen in red on the bottom of this Mirage IIIDE; the two Alkan-65 launchers for practice bombs, in the center line; two 449-gallon (1,700-liter) tanks; the barrels of the cannons; and above all, the excellent condition of the gray paint, which could mean that the aircraft had recently undergone a *grand visite*. *(Revista de Aeronaútica y de Astronaútica)*

purchase of thirty aircraft, as well as the necessary spare parts and support equipment, with an option to buy another fifteen aircraft. At the same time, the idea was considered that these Mirage III aircraft could be assembled in Spain by Construcciones Aeronáuticas in their factories in Getafe and Seville, as had been the recent case with seventy Northrop F-5 aircraft.

The process was very fast, as the signing of a protocol took place in Paris February 10th, an event that included the participation of the Spanish foreign minister and the French minister of defense, among other figures from both countries, as well as representatives from the Dassault company.

The document, which was inscribed "in the framework of technical and industrial cooperation in the matter of aeronautics," established the manufacture of thirty aircraft, the first batch of which would be delivered after a few months, with the final ones arriving in 1972.

In the meantime, the Air Force announced that these aircraft would have their base in Manises, where they would form a unit to cover the Mediterranean side of Spain. On February 26th, the Chief of Staff of the Air Force and the director general of Avions Marcel Dassault signed the final contract in Madrid with a total value of 6,300 million *pesetas*, equivalent to six million U.S. dollars (which would allow for the purchase of twenty-four single-seater Mirage IIIEE aircraft and six two-seater training Mirage IIIDE aircraft). At the same time, similar documents were signed with Manufacture de Machines du Haut-Rhin and with Engines Matra S.A. for the purchase of spare parts, equipment, and armaments for the aircraft. The documentation did not mention the assembly of these aircraft in Spain, as had been speculated on a few months previously; nonetheless, by means of parallel agreements between governments in both countries, industrial collaborations in the aeronautical area had been planned which went a long way towards compensating the investment.

At the beginning of March, a group of eight pilots and thirty maintenance specialists left Manises for France to adapt the new aircraft model, and continued to be responsible for this from the time they began to be delivered. These men were based at Dijon-Longvic air base and integrated into the *Escadron de Chasse 2/2 Côte d'Or*, where, with the French Mirage III aircraft, they began an intense period of training and familiarization with materiel and work methods that was very different from the North American ones they were used to.

The first aircraft

Due to the need demonstrated by the Air Force to use new flight material, as well as the interest

Next to this Mirage IIIEE, a crew member poses in a pressurized suit which allows him to carry out high-altitude flights if decompression occurs. *(Revista de Aeronaútica y de Astronaútica)*

by Dassault-Breguet in opening up a new market, they both convinced the Chief of Staff of the *Armée de l'Air* to deviate from the production line of the French aircraft and manufacture ten single-seater aircraft, the only ones out of a total of twenty-four that had French serial numbers: 580 to 582 and 591 to 597. This explains how they were able to supply Spain in such a short period of time.

On April 10th, the manufacturer delivered the three first Mirage IIIEE aircraft to the French base. These were given the serial numbers C.11-1/101-01, C.11-2/101-02, and C.11-3/101-03. Joining them in the following days were aircraft with the numbers C.11-4/101-04, C.11-5/101-05, C.11-6/101-06, C.11-7/101-07, C.11-8/101-08, C.11-9/101-09, and C.11-10/101-10. At the same time, the first of the six two-seaters with serial numbers CE.11-1/101-16 was transferred. These aircraft were passed into the hands of the Spanish pilots while training with the French two-seater aircraft was progressing.

At 11:40 on June 13th, after carrying out various fly-bys over the Manises base, the first of the Mirage IIIEE landed, piloted by Lieutenant Colonel José Rodríguez López, head of 101st Squadron; following him were Major José Parés of the Rosa and Captains José Pablo Guil Pijuan, Jerónimo Domínguez Palacín, Celso Juberías Martínez, José Luis Guallar Herránz, Eduardo González-Gallarza Morales, and Ángel Negrón Pezzi, the eight pilots who had trained for many months at the Dijon and Orange bases. They,

This Mirage III is landing and reducing its speed with the characteristic drogue parachute in a cruciform shape, very similar to those of the F1. *(Revista de Aeronaútica y de Astronaútica)*

in turn, passed on their experience to the rest of the crews that would be in charge of aircraft to be delivered over the next three years.

At the beginning, the Mirage III were posted to the 101st Squadron, which, until the end of February, had operated a certain number of F-86F Sabres. This organizational situation changed in May the following year (1971).

Meanwhile, at the end of the 1970s, the number of aircraft reached a dozen. These aircraft were in great use, as they combined the tasks of teaching with those of testing and weapon evaluation. They were often seen at the now-disused Caudé firing range, where air-to-ground sorties were carried out, and the air-to-air firing ranges where mock air battles were held.

Before the end of 1970, the first accident occurred, which resulted in a total loss of the aircraft. This happened December 16th, between Alcázar de San Juan and Heredia, in Ciudad Real, when, during a training mission and as a consequence of having started to spin, CE.11-1, with the crew of Captains José Pablo Guil Pijuán and Antonio García Lozano, had to use their ejector seats to abandon the aircraft, which then fell to the ground and was totally destroyed. This was, as will be seen later, the first of ten total losses suffered by the Mirage IIIEE and IIIDE during their many years of service.

The presence of military aircraft in civil airports is very common, as they are used as intermediate re-provisioning stages when travelling long distances. *(Revista de Aeronaútica y de Astronaútica)*

Line of Mirage III in Manises. It is worth pointing out the major's uniform, the covers of the pitot tube, and the fin at angle of attack. The number 21 showing on the flap of the landing gear corresponds to the serial number, as this is C.11-21. *(Revista de Aeronaútica y de Astronaútica)*

Low-altitude patrol flight by C-11.2/112-01 and a F-104G, an Italian military aircraft. The exchange of aircraft between allied countries is very common and extremely interesting from an operational point of view, as they allow for insights into different operating practices. *(Revista de Aeronaútica y de Astronaútica)*

The aircraft

The Mirage IIIEE — the second E standing for España (Spain) — was a much more advanced model manufactured from the IIIC, with a SNECMA Atar 09 C3 propeller engine giving it 9,480 lb (4,300 kg) thrust, becoming 13,669 lb (6,200 kg) with afterburner. It also differed from the IIIC version due to the extension of the front fuselage, which had grown 30 cm to allow space for the multifunction Thomson-CSF Cyrano 2b radar.

The internal armament was made up of two 30 mm DEFA 552 cannons, with a chamber capable of 125 rounds per weapon. It was able to carry the relevant supports for missiles, bombs, and auxiliary fuel tanks under its wings. In the case of the first aircraft, air-to-air short range AIM-9B Sidewinder weapons were used, which were later replaced by more advanced models, such as the AIM-9P. An air-to-air medium range MATRA R-530 missile launcher was able to fit under the fuselage, as well as infrared guiding, such as semi-active radar, which could only be distinguished from the outside by its seeker head. This weapon was able to be complemented by different types and weights of bombs, as well as LAU-32 rocket launchers, which held 18 68 mm weapons.

This aircraft, modern at the time, had, in addition to the radar already mentioned, an advanced electronics system made up of a Marconi-Elliot FR-100 Doppler navigation system and a Thomson-CSF 97 visor, which is considered the predecessor to the present-day HUD (Head up Display).

The IIIDE *Dual Espagne* was a dual control model suitable for being converted to operational use; however, it lacked radar and Doppler, and was therefore unsuitable for combat. It kept the pair of DEFA 552 cannons and the possibility of carrying two Sidewinder missiles.

The series is completed

After the arrival of the first ten single-seaters and the first of the six two-seaters, in September of the same year (1970) CE.11-25/101-17 arrived, and in July 1971 it was the turn of CE.11-26/101-18. A number of months went by — all of the following fall and part of the winter — before the bulk of the deliveries of aircraft manufactured specifically for Spain began, with the first to arrive being CE.11-27/103-16, which landed in Manises January 11, 1972; after which the rest of the aircraft arrived gradually, but not in the order of the

C.11-22, 112-11 has used the arrester net during a landing in Manises. Its use, in extreme cases, always caused damage to the weak parts of the aircraft, such as the antennas and underwing supports. *(Revista de Aeronaútica y de Astronaútica)*

September 14, 1979, when C.11-11/111-6 landed at Manises and, as a result of a failure of the landing gear, caught fire. It was withdrawn from service, as it was not considered cost effective to repair it. *(Revista de Aeronaútica y de Astronaútica)*

Although this image is not of a Spanish aircraft or base, it is extremely interesting, as it shows the performance of a detection net similar to that in Manises. (*Marcel Dassault*)

registrations: one in March (CE.11-28/103-17); three in April (C.11-12/ 112-6, C.11-11/111-6, and CE.11-29/103-18); one in May (C.11-15/103-03); and three in June (C.11-13/103-01, C.11-14/103-02, and C.11-16/103-04). In July the same year, five aircraft were delivered (C.11-17/103-05, C.11-18/103-06, C.11-19/103-07, C.11-20/103-08, and C.11-21/103-09), while the last three arrived in October (C.11-22/103-10, C.11-23/103-11, and C.11-24/103-12).

As a result of the loss of CE.11.1, the Air Force ordered one more two-seater aircraft, to be delivered July 25, 1973. This brought the total number of Mirage IIIEE and IIIDE actually flown by the Spanish air force to thirty-one aircraft. This replacement, which happened in a very short space of time, is not always picked up on by those who have written about the Mirage III, sticking to the total initial figure of thirty aircraft.

Genealogy of the Ala 11

This unit, the first Spanish one with turbojet aircraft, was created September 6, 1955, as *Ala de Caza* (Fighter Wing) no. 1 by means of an official order. The allocated aircraft were fifty North American F-86F Sabre aircraft, the legendary fighter planes from Korea. The *Ala*

consisted of a rare occurrence up until that time: two Squadrons (11 and 12), each with twenty-five aircraft. To distinguish between them, the pilots chose red and blue to use as bands on the noses of the aircraft. The 11th Squadron had red bands and answered to the radio code *Condor*, while the 12th used blue and the name *Dolar*. These colors stayed with the Mirage III until its withdrawal from *Ala 11* October 1992. As a result of the Mirage III being camouflaged,

these colors disappeared from the fuselages; however, they continued to be used in the insignias of the squadrons.

Months later, at the end of 1956, the unit saw a reduction in its number of aircraft, because twenty-four of its Sabres were sent to the Son San Juan base as part of the recently-created *Ala de Caza* no. 4. They stayed there for nine years, until the unit was disbanded in 1965, meaning that the aircraft returned to Manises

in April 1965 to be integrated into the 111th and 112th squadrons, which had the *Ala de Caza* at that time. As a result of an organizational change, the unit was in the process of being renamed *Ala de Caza* no. 11. Shortly afterwards the 111th Squadron was renamed the 101st Squadron.

As a result of a new strategic change, in October 1965, the Air Force divided its combat forces between the recently-created Defense

A Mirage F1 of Ala 14, an F-4C Phantom of Ala 12, and an F-5 of the 731st Squadron of Talavera are flying next to a Mirage IIIEE of Ala 11. *(Revista de Aeronaútica y de Astronaútica)*

Command and the Tactical Command, turning *Ala* no. 11 into a multi-role unit with a Squadron (111th) under the authority of the Tactical Command for immediate support missions and ground attacks, and the 101st assigned to the Aerial Defense Command. These two were the successors of the 11th and 12th, which for many years had *Ala de Caza* no. 1. In February 1967, the 111th Squadron was disbanded, leaving just the 101st active to carry out the air defense tasks

from that time and until the Mirage IIIEE was in full use. In November of the same year, the 101st Squadron became an independent unit assigned to Manises air base and *Ala* 11 disappeared temporarily; this continued until February 1970, when the Sabre aircraft stopped carrying out warning services and the unit was deactivated.

With the arrival of the first Mirage III, the 101st Squadron became active again after a

dozen of the new French aircraft had been operating alone. When the time was approaching to receive the rest of the aircraft, by means of a ministerial order included in the Official Bulletin of June 3, 1971, *Ala* 11 was created, and the 111th Squadron named as the unit to receive the aircraft. Shortly afterwards a new squadron, the 103rd Squadron, became active, although it had a very short lifespan, because as set down in document no. 878/3300 on

October 28, 1971, it was replaced by the 112th, which became active January 12, 1972. In June of the same year the two squadrons were complete.

Coding

Throughout most of the twenty-two years of service, each of the squadrons kept twelve single-seater Mirage IIIEE and three two-seater IIIDE active. These aircraft had registrations C.11-1 to C.11-24 for the single-seaters and CE.11-25 to CE.11-30 for the training two-seaters. As far as the latter are concerned, it should be made clear that the first training aircraft, which had the accident December 16, 1970, according to some authors had the registration CE.11-16, while others state it was CE.11-1. Regarding the unit codes, during the first months and until the creation of the 111th and 112th squadrons, the aircraft in service had the unit codes 101-01 to 101-10 for the single-seaters, and 101-16 for the two-seaters, respectively. After the appearance of the two squadrons these codes changed, meaning that the aircraft with odd-numbered registrations were incorporated into the 111th Squadron (C.11-1/111-1, C.11-3/111-2, etc.), while those with even-numbered plates were assigned to the 112th Squadron (C.11-2/112-1, C.11-4/112-

View of the underneath of a Mirage IIIEE. In front of the main landing gear there is the dielectric fairing of the antenna of the Doppler Thomson CSF radar, which allows the exact flight altitude to be known. In the center are the main landing gear flaps, with their characteristic angle position. This aircraft carries 158-gallon (600-liter) underwing tanks. *(Pere Redón)*

A patrol made up of four aircraft. All of them carry 158-gallon (600-liter) fuel tanks. On the back of the planes, the red brake flaps can be seen clearly against the dark camouflage background. *(Revista de Aeronaútica y de Astronaútica)*

2, etc.). The aircraft that arrived from April 1972 onwards initially had the codes of the 103ʳᵈ Squadron, and shortly afterwards they had these codes. In the case of the two-seaters, the first of these did not have the new codes; this only happened with the second and third of these aircraft, as they had been delivered in September 1970 and July 1971, meaning that, for a time, they used the codes 101-17 and 101-18. The remaining four, which were incorporated between January 1972 and July 1973, arrived with the codes of the 103ʳᵈ Squadron and, a little later, the new numbering (111-14, 112-14, 111-15, and 112-15, respectively).

From the beginning of 1987, and as a result of the application of a new rule related to the unifying of all unit codes, the Air Force issued an order by which:

...all the aircraft will carry on their fuselage, preferably on the nose, two numbers separated by the roundel: one pertaining to the unit they belong to, and the other to their order within this unit. The number relating to the unit, made up of two digits, will be that which corresponds to the Ala they are assigned to, meaning the airplanes will cease to belong to the Squadrons. The independent Squadrons will continue to keep three digits. The numbers of the order, also of two digits, will serve to distinguish the

aircraft of the same Unit by type and model. Therefore, those numbered 01 to 49 will be for the basic aircraft of the Unit; those from 50 to 69 will be for the special version; those from 70 to 89 for dual control models; and those from 90 to 99 will be for other types not specified previously.

This ruling also covered other aspects, amongst them the reduction of the size of the roundels and St. Andrew's Cross and coding for less visibility. It was in this period that the aerial units of other countries painted false cabins on the underneath of the fuselage. In the Air Force, this was only adopted by some C.14 aircraft.

As a result of this ruling coming into effect, the Mirage III changed its old coding in line with the new law. The single-seaters were thus renumbered 11-01 to 11-24, and the two-seaters from 11-70 to 11-75. Numbers 11-07, 11-11, 11-12, 11-14, 11-19, and 11-20 were not used, as they corresponded to aircraft that had been withdrawn due to accidents before the application of this new law. These codes showed on the fuselages up until the time that the Mirage III aircraft were taken out of service.

Activity and flight hours

Once the coding of *Ala* 11 was finished, and after a long period of training to find out what the aircraft had to offer, on February 11, 1973, the unit underwent an assessment by the leaders

Front view of C.11-23. The air brakes can be seen on the back of the wings and in the middle. Behind the aircraft is the arrester net at Manises. *(Pere Redón)*

of the Air Force, an exercise that included both land and air stages. During the first stages, the pilots took written exams covering logistical and technical aspects, while the second proved their operational performance by means of a *Red-Eye* aerial defense exercise.

Over the following years, and until this aircraft was withdrawn, *Ala* 11 was in charge of carrying out aerial defense missions and ground attacks. Within the general area of scramble aerial defense, medium, low, and high level interception missions were developed, high night speeds, and aerial combat between Mirage III aircraft and against other types of aircraft. The framework where most of these practices were carried out was the LE-D-26 firing range in the south of Ibiza. In this area, where aerial and maritime navigation were prohibited, they used both internal and external weapons consisting of the pair of 30mm DEFA cannons and the AIM-9 Sidewinder missiles, as well as the Matra R-530. The air-to-land missions were made up of machine-gunning, bombing, totally independent navigations at high and low level, rocket launching, armed reconnaissance with mock attacks, and photographic reconnaissance carried out with an Omera 60 camera. The combinations of underwing jettisonable weapons assigned to each of the missions were able to reach up to a maximum of 2,000 kilos, although this figure could be higher, but at a cost to the fuel load capacity, and in turn the radius of action.

During an open day at Manises, the aircraft are displaying all the offensive armaments that could be loaded on a Mirage IIIEE. *(Revista de Aeronaútica y de Astronaútica)*

This capacity meant that, throughout its operational life, it participated fully in *Red-Eye* exercises for aerial defense; *Pop-Deck*, which was coastal defense against external attacks from North American aircraft of the USAF and the U.S. Navy, with subsequent tracking down and attack on aircraft carriers; *NAVIPAR*, or exchange with French aerial defense; *Barrage* and *Datex*, to assess the French aerial defense; and in others, such as *Crisex, DACT*, and *Helios-Aries*. From 1983, after Spain's entry into NATO, *Ala* 11, among other Spanish units, began to undertake exchanges with fighter and attack units in other countries of the Treaty. These usually lasted around ten days, during which time both those travelling to the aerial bases, as well as the foreigners who were being integrated into *Ala* 11, undertook all types of training missions.

The experience accumulated over the thousands of missions carried out showed that the Mirage III was an excellent interceptor, capable of successfully facing many of the aircraft of its first era. Its success was assured at supersonic speeds and above thirty thousand feet. As far as air-land missions were concerned, penetration at low and very low levels was always undertaken with considerable advantages, considering that it was a ground-attack aircraft that always had some very particular characteristics.

In the context of the real missions, it should be said that the Mirage IIIEE of *Ala* 11 began

C.11-22 on the aircraft stand at Manises. On the dark background of the fuselage, the insignia of *Ala* 11, with its motto, *Vista, suerte y al toro* ("A glance, luck and at the bull") can be seen. *(Revista de Aeronaútica y de Astronaútica)*

to undertake warning service on March 26, 1973. By means of weekly shifts, each squadron kept two aircraft on constant alert, the first for a five minute take off and a second with a thirty minute preparation. With the APU (auxiliary power unit) connected, and armed and ready with two air-to-air Sidewinder missiles, both aircraft waited for the alarm signal to undertake an interception/identification mission. This service stayed active without interruptions until March 14, 1989. During this period of almost seventeen years, the Mirage IIIEE carried out more than four hundred scrambles or immediate takeoffs.

The Achilles heel of the Mirage III was the elevated speed of stall between 140 and 160 knots, which translated into the difficult and very fast landings that necessitated the obligatory use of drogue parachutes, as well as the use of supplementary security measures of an arrester net situated at the end of the 9,843-foot (3,000-meter) long runway at Manises. Despite the precautions, a number of the incidents and accidents suffered by the Mirage were due to this factor.

The operational activity of this reduced group of aircraft was always very evident, and as a consequence, flight hours were quickly accumulated. In August 1972, they had racked up 5,000 hours, and by December 12th the following year they had completed their first 10,000. This latter landmark was achieved within the framework of a normal period of

Two-seater trainer CE.11-27/111-14. Its main external characteristic stems from the elongated nose that contains part of the electronics and a graphic reconnaissance camera, which is situated in the backseat space in single-seaters. In the centerline, there are two Alkan-65 launchers for practice bombs. Along the target leading edge, under the aircraft's serial number, there is a thin stabilizing fin that is only fitted on two-seaters. (*Revista de Aeronaútica y de Astronaútica*)

training, in which various night intercept missions had been planned. After aircraft C.11-20, piloted by Captain Carlos Gómez Mira, had just carried out a frontal face-to-face interceptor mission guided by the Constantina Squadron of Warning and Control – the present day EVA-3– it had reached 10,000 hours. Over time these records were beaten, reaching 25,000 hours on August 31, 1977; 30,000 on October 10, 1978; 40,000 on January 5, 1981; 50,000 on May 3, 1983; 60,000 on August 2, 1985; 70,000 on December 15, 1987; and by October 1992, when they were taken out of service, they had accumulated more than 80,000 hours with the loss of only ten aircraft, equaling a rate of one aircraft for every 8,000 flight hours, and indicative of the extraordinary level of safety of these aircraft.

Incidents and accidents

When the operational life of a combat aircraft is discussed, it is inevitable that reference be made to the negative aspects, such as the loss of aircraft and pilots. This is something that the crew of the units, including the maintenance specialists, accept, in spite of one of the daily pre-flight briefings being related to flight security. Another of the factors which is always looked at are the accident prevention programs via improved teaching, breakdown prevention, and the improvement of maintenance, but despite this enormous effort, incidents and accidents are inevitable.

This angled view allows for some of the details of the back of the wings and the fuselage to be seen. It shows off the fusiform shape and the stabilizing fins of the 449-gallon (1,700-liter) tank, the port air brake, the inlet on this side, and on the central part of the body, the small air inlet for the air cooling system. (Pere Redón)

The first of the total losses took place December 16, 1970, when the only two-seater which existed at that time, CE.11-1, began spinning and was unable to stop, forcing the two members of the crew to jump. The next accident happened November 19, 1974, after a gap of almost four years; on this occasion it was C.11-14, and its crew were killed. On May 5, 1977, C.11-7 entered the recoil area of the aircraft in front during a take-off in formation, causing -7 to do a half barrel roll and crash on the runway; even though the pilot stayed with the aircraft so that it was held by the barrier, he could not stop the plane catching fire. The pilot escaped unharmed, but the aircraft was left in such a bad state that it was declared irreparable. On May 8, 1978, C.11-19 crashed and the pilot jumped. C.11-20 fell into the Mediterranean opposite Denia on July 14, 1978, during a mission and the pilot was killed. The next accident happened September 14, 1979, when C.11-11 was lost during a landing in Manises, with the aircraft considered beyond repair. During a shooting mission on the firing range of Bardenas Reales, C.11-12 was brought down by the rebound of its own missiles, but the pilot survived. C.11-30 was the two-seater that was bought to replace the one lost in 1970. On May 20, 1978, this aircraft, in turn, also started to spin when it was flying over the Mediterranean opposite Denia, forcing the crew to jump. On July 11, 1991, C.11-15 was lost on the landing at Manises due to failure of the

CE.11-27 taxiing on the apron towards the take off point. On the nose, and in front of the cabin, there are two small horn-shaped pressure regulators.
(Revista de Aeronaútica y de Astronaútica)

left lander, and even though it was considered reparable, the aircraft was withdrawn due to the forthcoming withdrawal of the Mirage III. The last of the accidents occurred February 3, 1992, when C.11-13 came off the runway during a landing, suffering significant damage that meant its repair was not justifiable.

Given the circumstances of some of the accidents, it was possible to opportunistically recover some elements for later use, mainly the engines, weapons, and instruments. One of the aircraft was recovered and later adapted and set up as a monument near the Manises control tower. It was C.11-7, an aircraft which, when the base was closed, went to the City of the Arts and Sciences in Valencia.

Inspections in France

When the purchase contract for the thirty Mirage was signed in 1970, this included a series of clauses that covered the training courses for the pilots and mechanics, and even the obtaining of spare parts and the undertaking in the neighboring country of what the French call a *grand visite*, because CASA had no experience in the maintenance of combat aircraft of that type.

Nine years after the arrival of the first aircraft and the accumulation of flight hours, the Mirage

This image shows the delta wing shape of the Mirage III. The shape, which is reminiscent of a plank, led to its nickname in Spanish "Plancheta." The ventral 132-gallon (500-liter) tank can also be seen. Joined to the fuselage are the two 158-gallon (600-liter) underwing tanks and the fairing of the actuator of the internal and external elevons. *(Revista de Aeronaútica y de Astronaútica)*

IIIEE began to move towards France in stages in 1979, so that they could undergo third level inspections — the corresponding *grand visite* overhaul, which would put the fleet at practically zero hours. It was at this point that the Air Force considered the possible purchase of twenty more of this type selected from the French aircraft, to strengthen the effectiveness of *Ala* 11. The acquisition did not materialize, because the French were only prepared to offer its older Mirage IIIC models with an overall capacity less than the Manises IIIEE.

The next *grand visite*, which was due to take place ten years later was, logically enough, called off when the modernization program was cancelled, at a time when the Air Force decided not to invest any money in this process, and as a consequence decided to plan for its deactivation, which took place in October 1992.

Aircraft in action

Over a twenty-three year span there were many events of all types in which these fighter aircraft were involved. Consequently, *Ala* 11 and its Mirage III experienced many tense moments, including the deployment in Gando and El Aiun of a detachment of four, where one aircraft broke a part of its main landing gear during a landing when supporting the Spanish forces of the Sahara.

Line of Mirage IIIEE during refueling from a tanker truck. In front of 11-04 there is one of the bicycles used by ground personnel to vacate the aircraft departure areas. The pitot tube, with its characteristic shape, can be seen in the foreground. *(Revista de Aeronaútica y de Astronaútica)*

In the fall of 1975 a dozen aircraft, along with their crews and support personnel, were in a state of alert for a number of days in case their presence was called for in that area. Fortunately, the *Green March* did not entail too much risk, and the Spanish evacuation was carried out with no further emotion than that involved in leaving the area behind.

Another action in which the unit was involved was the bombing of the Cypriot ship *Northern Star*, which was carrying chemicals when it strayed to the south of the Balearic Islands. On this occasion, four Phantoms from *Ala* 12 and four Mirage IIIEE aircraft were dispatched to bomb and sink the ship using Mk 117 bombs, 70 mm rockets, and munitions from the internal cannons.

When the deactivation of aircraft, and consequently its load of Matra R-530 missiles were approaching, the order was given for its use in a shooting exercise against reflective targets, an action that was carried out for the first and only time.

On other occasions related to another type of action, *Ala* 11 was often on call so that various Mirage III aircraft could escort national and foreign aircraft that were transporting dignitaries visiting Spain, with one of the most notable being the Pope in October 1992.

Two mechanics carrying out a pre-flight inspection at daybreak. The reflection of the sun on the fuselage shows how the camouflage has deteriorated.
(Pere Redón)

Exchanges with Argentina

Within the normal framework of exchange of pilots from different Air Force units with units from other countries, during the years 1982 and 1984, various components of *Ala* 11 flew in fighter Groups 6 and 8 of the Argentinean Air Force, while pilots from these units stayed in Manises for some months. Nonetheless, the decisive moment of exchange with Argentina took place in 1992, as a result of the limited number of flight hours which the Argentineans were able to undertake, meaning eight pilots from Group 6 were invited to stay in the 111th Squadron for a month, during which time they were totally integrated so as to be able to carry out normal missions together with the Spanish.

Interrupted modernization

With the aim of prolonging the operational life of these excellent aircraft, in November 1987, the Air Force announced it was planning to carry out significant modernization of the fleet with the intention of achieving, amongst other things, the improvement of the combat capacity against land targets, the possibility of in-flight refueling, and updating the radar. In terms of the propulsion engine, the project included a level three inspection of the engine and putting it back to zero flight hours. In terms of the

C.11-3 shows the condition of the protective paint. Its deterioration allows for all the registrations of the starboard side to be made out. In the forefront, in white, is one of the rails transporting a Sidewinder. *(Revista de Aeronaútica y de Astronaútica)*

structure of the aircraft, they would incorporate aerodynamic improvements to allow for the increase of the pattern of instant and sharp turns at all heights, both for air-surface as well as air-to-air. These changes would also increase the flight quality, especially for air-to-air, and the capacity to take off with maximum load and at elevated temperatures. The Cyrano radar would be improved or changed, and the aircraft would receive a telemetric laser for air-to-surface operations.

An investment of twenty billion *pesetas* (roughly $157,000,000) was planned, a figure that did not include the creation of programs for the new computer, as this would be covered by another budget. The time frame for the length of the work was estimated at four years, with an annual cost of five billion *pesetas* per year.

The company involved was Israel Aircraft Industries (IAI), which offered the development of a prototype in its country of origin, and the proposal that CASA would undertake the main part of the work, a company that would have the then-named CESELSA, today known as INDRA, as subcontractor. CASA immediately abandoned the project due to political and commercial reasons related to the costs. After

C.11-3/11-03 with the fairing of the dorsal radio and avionics compartment lifted up. Inside are: the VHF receptor/ transmitter systems; Doppler transceiver; aerial data computer; missile encoder; altimeter transceiver; inertial correction computer; and armament connection box. In the two-seaters, most of the instruments are fitted in the nose. In the next compartment, which is also open, are the air conditioning pipes and cooling system filters. (Revista de Aeronaútica y de Astronaútica)

Four personnel of Ala 11 install an AIM-9 Sidewinder port underwing pylon. The blue color of this device means that it is a static weapon of a type used in air-to-air exercises. *(Revista de Aeronaútica y de Astronaútica)*

This mechanic is getting ready to place the parabrake container in its compartment on the reactor outlet nozzle. *(Pere Redón)*

this separation CASA joined with Marcel Dassault, while IAI joined with CESELSA. Over the following months, a real economic and political battle was fought for the contract, during which time some rather unorthodox methods were employed. During this time, the Air Force continued to dictate all the elements, instruments, and methods to be changed, and therefore some delays were caused in the final decision making. Meanwhile, the Mirage III went through a period of low activity as a result of the lack of spare parts. This was due to the fact that, at the beginning, when its withdrawal was being considered, the supply channel of spare parts was cancelled, with stock remaining only up to January 1988. A large number of aircraft were taken out of service temporarily for two months.

In May 1988, the Spanish Ministry of Defense, in view of the continual delays and doubts, steered the formation of a partnership between CASA and CESELSA. The signing of the agreement for the creation of an independent management society called ATTORN took place at the end of December 1988, but despite this, the horizon continued to be plagued by problems that were not resolved during either 1989 or 1990. The apparent lack of interest, industrial problems, and external pressures meant that the Ministry intervened on a number of occasions, even threatening to cancel the contract and return the first payment of 5 billion *pesetas*. It also warned that the participation of both companies would be hindered in other awards. In November 1990, and in agreement, CASA and CESELSA proposed the deactivation of ATTORN to the Ministry and put themselves forward as contractor and subcontractor, respectively, which, as the lesser evil, was accepted. Despite this the problems continued, leading the Ministry to permanently cancel the program that it had already invested six billion in on August 6, 1991, claiming that the decision was taken in view of the inability of the two Spanish companies to carry on. It also came to light that France and Israel had contributed to the interruptions suffered by the project, as they had thought they could escape the monopoly exhibited by the modernization of this type of aircraft present in various countries, which sooner or later would have to be part of a program similar to the Spanish one.

Withdrawal and final destination

The decision not to modernize the aircraft came together with the decision to withdraw them from service, an action which was planned to

At Manises, it was very common to have group takeoffs. These two IIIDE two-seaters are going on a training flight. *(Pere Redón)*

take place June 30, 1992, but was later delayed until October 1st of the same year. The last flights therefore took place on September 30th, a sad day for the personnel of *Ala* 11. Five flights were planned that day to the Caudé firing range in Teruel, where the small inactive bombs they were carrying were released.

Afterwards, the twenty-one aircraft still in service — sixteen single-seaters and five two-seaters — were moved to Getafe air base, where they stayed for a number of years with all the openings covered and the cabins covered by protective canvas, waiting for a buyer, but this did not materialize.

When the contract was signed for the modernization of the Mirage F1, the Air Force included a clause stating that it was offering this batch of aircraft in addition to the financial amount stated, a clause that was accepted by the French company Thomson-CSF, meaning that the Mirage became its property, with the expectation that they would be resold or dismantled and the components used as spare parts.

Although talks were set up with Argentina, which had a similar version, these did not produce any results. In the end, fifteen aircraft were transferred with a batch of similar aircraft from the *Armée de l'Air* to Pakistan, which used them for spare parts. It appears that the

Filling up the JP-4 fuel tanks of C.11-10.
(Revista de Aeronaútica y de Astronaútica)

other six went to the AMIO company, although their final destination is unknown.

C.11-9, a complete aircraft, is in the Air Museum at Cuatro Vientos, as well as the fuselage of C.11-13. C.11-7, which is on display in the aforementioned City of the Arts and Sciences in Valencia, is the same one that was located at the foot of the Manises control tower for some years.

Heraldry

The long-established tradition of giving shields to aircraft meant that, with the creation of *Ala de Caza* No. 1, the insignia of the muzzled hyena was born, along with the motto *Se alimenta de carroña, se aparea una vez al año, y aún se ríe* ("Feeds on carrion, mates once a year, and still laughs"). This animal figured for many years on the fuselages of the Sabre and

on the overalls of the pilots, on a half blue and half red background. Later on in 1959, and set down in a decree on 17 February, the Chief of Staff designated the *Ala* as receiver of the tradition of Spanish hunting represented by the former García Morato Group. From that time on, the official insignia of the unit consisted of three birds (Falcon, Bustard, and Blackbird), a laurel wreath, and the motto *Vista, suerte y al*

This Mirage IIIEE is taking off at Manises with the combustion activated. These aircraft never used the lift jets. (*Revista de Aeronaútica y de Astronaútica*)

toro ("Vision, luck and the bull"), an insignia that in a simplified form also figured prominently on the aircraft of that period (the F-86F T-33). On April 4, 1959, the handing over of the corresponding standard on which the aforementioned shield appeared gave rise to some discussion in relation to the hyena, which was going to disappear. This discussion was resolved by the head of the unit, who delivered the phrase *Ese, que no valga* ("That has no worth"), and so the old motto temporarily disappeared and was replaced by the new one, *Que no valga* ("No worth").

The arrival of the Mirage III showing the logical camouflage did not break with the old heraldic tradition, even if next to the aircraft's registration code only the insignia of the recently created *Ala* 11 appeared, leaving the shields of the squadrons just for the pilots' flight overalls. This was the point at which the hyena was brought back into use, together with the scathing phrase of the 111th Squadron – even if it was on a blue background – leaving that of the bat carrying a Matra R-530 missile for the 112th Squadron on a red background.

C.11-7/111-4, which, due to an accident, was rebuilt and installed (next to an F-86F Sabre) in front of the Manises control building. When the aircraft was broken up and the base dismantled, the aircraft was given to the City of Arts and Sciences in Valencia. *(Pere Redón)*

Ala 11

111th Squadron

112th Squadron

112th Squadron

CE.11-27 ready for a training flight. The characteristic noses of these aircraft contain a graphic reconnaissance camera. *(Revista de Aeronaútica y de Astronaútica)*

Mirage IIIEE

Mirage IIIDE

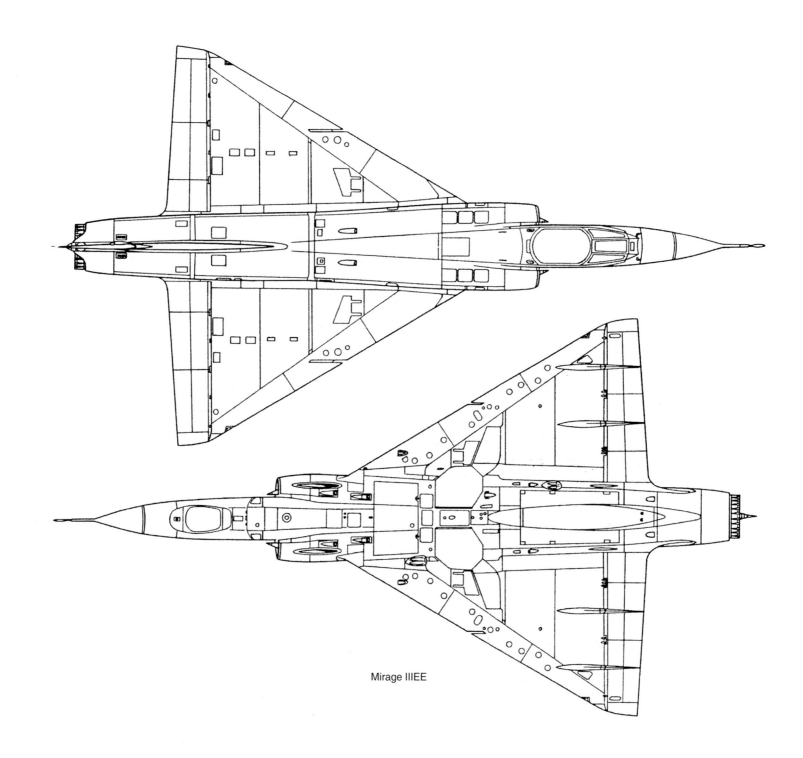

Mirage IIIEE

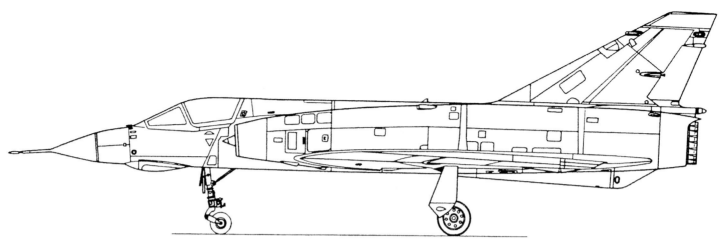

MIRAGE III EE/DE: TECHNICAL SPECIFICATIONS

Dimensions		Weight	
Wingspan	8.22	Empty weight	7,050 kg m
Length	14.15 m (C-11)	Maximum take-off weight	13,500 kg
	15.03 m (CE-11)	Wing load	370 kg/m^2
Height	4.25 m	**Fuel**	
Wing area	34.85 m2	Maximum internal capacity	3,300 l
Sweep	60º	Drop tanks	in the central and inner parts with capacities of 500, 600, 1,300, and 1,700 l

Performance			
Maximum speed to 12,000 m	Mach 2.2	Service ceiling at Mach 1.8	17,000 m
Maximum speed to sea level	Mach 1.3	Take-off roll	700/1,800 m depending on load
Cruising speed to 11,000 m	Mach 0.9	Landing roll	700 m with chute
Landing speed	300 km/h	Operational range, with internal fuel	600 km
Climbing speed	200 m/sec	Operational range, with tanks	2,300 km

Armament *situated at 5 hardpoints*			
Internal	2 DEFA 5-52 30 mm cannons with 125 rounds per gun		
Missiles	1 MATRA R.530 missile, *center of fuselage*	Various low resistance bombs	
	2 AIM-9, Sidewinder missiles, *various types*	Various combinations of rockets	

Power		Electronic equipment	
Engine	1 SNECMA Atar 9C turbojet with 6,200 kg afterburner thrust	Cyrano II B exploration and shooting radar .	
		Doppler ground mapping radar.	
		Radar alarms. UHF and VHF radio equipment. Firing solution	

The interrupted renovation of the Mirage III would have meant the adoption of an in-flight fueling system, the installation of additional points for carrying armaments, and above all, it would have been fitted with advanced avionics and high technology cabin instruments.
(Dassault Aviation)

AIR FORCE MIRAGE IIIEE / DE: ADMINISTRATIVE PLAN

Air Force	Armée Air	Date of Delivery	Code up to 3/1971	Code 1972	Code 5/1971-1987	Code 1987-1992	Withdrawal Date	Withdrawal Due to Accident
C.11-1	580	09.04.70	101-01	—	111-1	11-01	(1) 15.02.90	—
C.11-2	581	09.04.70	101-02	—	112-1	11-02	(1) 15.03.89	—
C.11-3	582	09.04.70	101-03	—	111-2	11-03	(1) 05.06.90	—
C.11-4	591	10.04.70	101-04	—	112-2	11-04	(2) 01.10.92	—
C.11-5	592	10.04.70	101-05	—	111-3	11-05	(1) 05.04.90	—
C.11-6	593	17.04.70	101-06	—	112-3	11-06	(2) 15.10.92	—
C.11-7	594	17.04.70	101-07	—	111-4	—	—	02.05.77 (3)
C.11-8	595	20.04.70	101-08	—	112-4	11-08	(2) 01.10.92	—
C.11-9	596	20.04.70	101-09	—	111-5	11-09	(1) 09.03.89 (4)	—
C.11-10	597	20.04.70	101-10	—	112-5	11-10	(2) 01.10.92	—
C.11-11	—	19.04.72	—	—	111-6	—	—	14.09.79
C.11-12	—	14.04.72	—	—	112-6	—	—	07.08.79
C.11-13	—	09.06.72	—	103-01	111-7	11-13	—	03.02.92 (5)
C.11-14	—	20.06.72	—	103-02	112-7	—	—	19.11.74
C.11-15	—	26.05.72	—	103-03	111-8	11-15	—	11.07.91 (6)
C.11-16	—	20.06.72	—	103-04	112-8	11-16	(1) 22.07.91	—
C.11-17	—	20.07.72	—	103-05	111-9	11-17	(2) 01.10.92	—
C.11-18	—	20.07.72	—	103-06	112-9	11-18	(2) 01.10.92	—
C.11-19	—	27.07.72	—	103-07	111-10	—	—	08.05.78
C.11-20	—	27.07.72	—	103-08	112-10	—	—	14.07.78
C.11-21	—	27.07.72	—	103-09	111-11	11-21	(2) 01.10.92	—
C.11-22	—	11.10.72	—	103-10	112-11	11-22	(2) 01.10.92	—
C.11-23	—	11.10.72	—	103-11	111-12	11-23	(2) 23.10.92	—
C.11-24	—	11.10.72	—	103-12	112-12	11-24	(2) 01.10.92	—
CE.11-1	—	10.04.70	101-16	—	—	—	—	16.12.70
CE.11-25	—	23.09.70	101-17	—	111-13	11-70	(2) 01.10.92	—
CE.11-26	—	—.07.71	101-18	—	112-13	11-71	(1) 20.11.89	—
CE.11-27	—	11.01.72	—	103-16	111-14	11-72	(2) 01.10.92	—
CE.11-28	—	30.03.72	—	103-17	112-14	11-73	(2) 01.10.92	—
CE.11-29	—	20.04.72	—	—	111-15	11-74	(2) 01.10.92	—
CE.11-30	—	25.07.73	—	103-18	112-15	11-75	—	20.05.88 (6)

Notes: **(1)** for modernization; **(2)** storage; **(3)** on display at the City of Arts and Sciences in Valencia; **(4)** on display at the Air Museum, Cuatro Vientos; **(5)** Fuselage stored at the Air Museum, Cuatro Vientos; **(6)** These two aircraft had minor accidents, but due to the forthcoming withdrawal of the fleet repairing them was not justified.

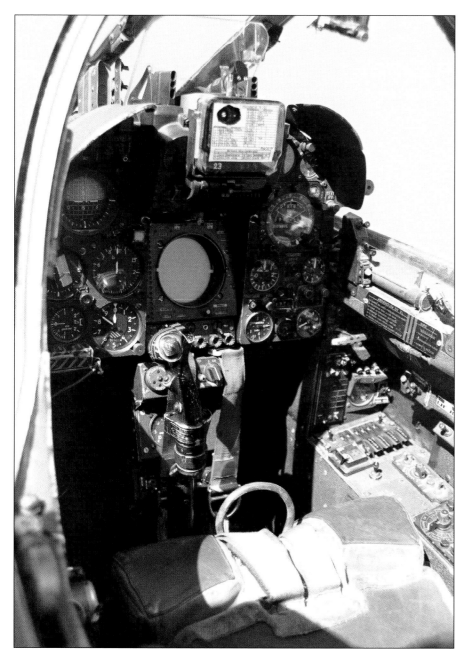

Inside the cockpit there are, amongst other instruments, the radar display, the control stick, the HUD, and the starboard panel. In the foreground is the ring which works the pyrotechnic ejection system for the ejector seat. *(Revista de Aeronaútica y de Astronaútica)*

Overall view of the cockpit of C.11-23/111-12. The upper part of the ejector seat with its harness and straps — removed before flying — can be seen; safety catches; the receptacle for the ring to take off the hood; the insignia of Ala 11; the port side air intake; and the pressure probe on this side. On the lower part, the fairing of the Doppler radar can be seen. After the number 12 is the red triangle that indicates the aircraft has an ejector seat. *(Pere Redón)*

This mechanic is One of the Thomson-CSF Cyrano II radars on a trolley; these were fitted on single-seaters. *(Revista de Aeronaútica y de Astronaútica)* getting ready to place the parabrake container in its compartment on the reactor outlet nozzle. *(Pere Redón)*

The vertical stabilizer of C.11-2 shows on the leading edge, starting from the top, the dielectric fairing of the VHF antenna; lower down, the passive radar antenna; and, in front of the serial number and cover, a small fairing of the UHF antenna. Also see at the back are the navigation lights – red for port and green for starboard – and the white anti-collision flash lights. The radar alarm, in the shape of a semi-circle on the St Andrew's Cross, and lower down the rudder actuator. Above the outlet nozzle there is the fairing housing the parabrake container. The moving pieces at the exit of the nozzle can be clearly seen. *(Pere Redón)*

Vertical rudder with front and back antennas and BDU radar threat warning system. *(Revista de Aeronaútica y de Astronaútica)*

Overview of the front and main landing gear, and the flaps which close the wheel wells. One of the sets of steps providing access to the cabin (always yellow) is on the ground. *(Pere Redón)*

One of the main landing gear wheels. Each strut supports the hydraulic ducts. *(Pere Redón)*

Matra R-530 missile with the relevant instructions for its use and connections. *(Revista de Aeronaútica y de Astronaútica)*

Left photographic camera of a Mirage III integrated into the keel formed by the fuel tank. *(Revista de Aeronaútica y de Astronaútica)*

Radioelectric hood covering the Marconi-Elliot Doppel navigator. Perpendicular to this, the front cover of the front landing gear can be seen with its indicators: the left side belongs to the electronic system working the strut, and the right side, the double rolling corresponding to the cooler. *(Revista de Aeronaútica y de Astronaútica)*

This is one of the tow targets used by the Mirage IIIEE for their cannon shooting practice, although they were usually carried by an F-4C Phantom of Ala 12. They have a simple construction consisting of a container/reel, nylon cord, and the target itself built on a wood chip target covered in aluminum to reflect the radar waves. *(Pere Redón)*

In the central pylon there is an EXPAL BR-250 550-pound (250-kilo) low drag practice fuseless bomb. The flaps for the main landing gear can be seen on both sides. *(Pere Redón)*

RPK-10 132-gallon (500-liter) fuel tank with four anchoring points for BR-250, EXPAL 550-pound (250-kilo) low-resistance bombs. *(Pere Redón)*

A MATRA R-530 missile with semi-active radar head on a centerline pylon. These weapons were air-to-air and medium range. *(Pere Redón)*

The exterior underwing station fits an inactive AIM-9 Sidewinder air-to-air missile and its stand. *(Pere Redón)*

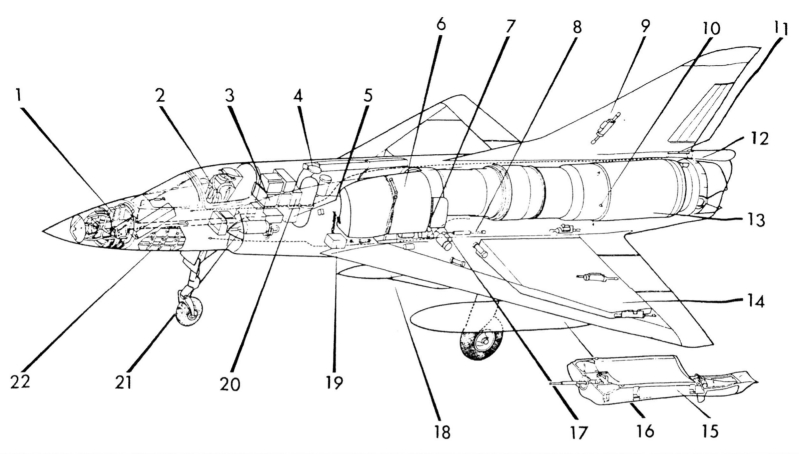

MIRAGE III, CROSS SECTION

1. Thomson CSF Cyrano II radar	**12.** Drogue parachute
2. Ejector seat, including sea survival equipment	**13.** SNECMA ATAR 9 C turbojets
3. UHF equipment	**14.** Fuel feed
4. Radio compass	**15.** SERP-841 support jets. (Air Force aircraft did not have them fitted)
5. General equipment, emergency brakes, central gyroscope, automatic height control, pressure regulator, etc.	**16.** Auxiliary drop tanks
6. Interior fuel tank	**17.** Hydraulic system
7. Fuel accessories	**18.** Matra R-530 missile
8. Elevator trim hydraulic pile driver	**19.** Electronic equipment
9. Hydraulic servo control on the three shafts	**20.** Electric generator
10. Fire detectors	**21.** Air conditioning equipment
11. Controls for opening or releasing parachutes	**22.** Structure, ribs, and longeron of the fuselage

Starboard side showing the air intake; inside it is the variable semi-conical central body. Between the air intake and the fuselage there is the opening that constitutes the dynamic pressure tube of the air conditioner. Under the fuselage there is a 158-gallon (600-liter) auxiliary drop tank. *(Pere Redón)*

The Mirage III are fitted with four air brakes: two in the upper part and the other two in the lower part. Above, there is the air brake with the sign "do not tread here." The two on the starboard side can be seen in the photograph on the left. *(Pere Redón)*

Assembly of the DEFA 552 30 mm ventral cannons, with their belt feed systems containing 125 shots per cannon. *(Pere Redón)*

The slot which allows the barrels of the cannons to protrude has rings that act as extinguishers. *(Pere Redón)*